INTJ.

UNDERSTAND AND BREAK
FREE FROM YOUR OWN
LIMITATIONS

MATTHEW BRIGHTHOUSE

Table of Contents

INTRODUCTION

Let me express my gratitude for the fact that you have you downloaded this book, *"INFJ: Understand And Break Free From Your Own Limitations"*.
Growing up as an INFJ isn't easy. Now that I'm older, I appreciate how resilient I have been throughout the years.

Most of the times, I felt lonely. In addition to that, I was always stressed. Although many referred to me as being calm, I was burning inside. And sadly, no one was there to listen to my troubles.

But like any INFJ, I never gave up. I went out of my way to work extra hard to ensure that my life improved and find inner peace. As years went on, I began to find the balance that had eluded me for so long. As you are reading this now, you may be going through the same problems.

In this book, I will show you how you can achieve inner peace. You will learn how to handle yourself at your workplace, the tips to fight negative emotions, fighting loneliness, how to achieve harmony and identify yourself as an INFJ.

This book is written specifically for passionate INFJs who need to do soul searching, pondering, reading, goal setting, opening their eyes and submerging into the subject of knowing themselves through the personality type INFJ. My quest for self-knowledge and self-development is essentially infinite. It will always spark my highest interest.

Those who carry the name of INFJ are <1%. However, this personality type can come with certain burdens. Shedding light on your distinct strengths and weaknesses gives you the ability to reflect, strengthen or re-evaluate certain aspects and choose to live your life confidently, your way.

INFJ is one of the 16 personality types described in the Myers-Briggs Type Indicator® (MBTI) personality tool developed by Isabel Briggs-Myers, and her mother, Katherine Briggs.

The purpose of the MBTI® is to further expand the theory of psychological types popularized by Carl Gustav Jung and make it more understandable and practical to use. The foundation of this theory is that the seemingly random variation in our personality is actually consistent and orderly, because of the essential differences in the ways people choose to respond according to their judgment and perception. Keep reading.

1
WHO IS AN INFJ

At this point, I'm going to assume you're an INFJ and reading about yourself, or reading about someone you care about who is an INFJ. I'm also going to assume you've read some of the basic descriptions online about INFJs and have bought this book because you want depth and details on how INFJs can thrive.

I'm not going to bore you with a lengthy or redundant description of an INFJ here. Rather, you will find some descriptions of INFJs from the leading schools of thought on type psychology.

INFJ is an abbreviation used to refer to one of the sixteen personality types in the Myer-Briggs Type Indicator (MBTI). In full, it means Introversion, Intuition, Feeling, and Judging.

This personality is unique as it is the rarest in the world. It makes just 1% of the population, with women being more than men.

1%. That's a small number, isn't it? We are extremely rare. At least that is what we are told. Imagine how you would feel if you are told that there is a 99% chance that the next person you meet is not like you. How would you feel? Deflated, to say the least. This feeds into the conception that INFJs often feel alone. One of our major difficulties in life is that we feel misunderstood, or at the very least, not reciprocated. Now imagine this! 1% out of 7.5 billion people. That is quite astounding. If we look at the number and do some math, we will find that if there are 1% of us, that actually means that we are potentially 75 million INFJs lurking around in this world (0.01 x

7,500,000,000 = 75,000,000)! If we were to collect them all into one geographical space, imagine how much land we would encompass. A village, town, city or even a small country would not even be able to contain us! This is quite an amazing realization. We are certainly not alone. Even if we do feel like we are at times.

We are a personality type that thrives on idealism. We love the idea that the world can rise to meet its potential. Our vision is a universal kindness to each other through the realization that we are all interconnected. Values of honesty, democracy, independence, and tolerance for one another is strong and evident throughout our being.

Envisioning a movement towards this perceived topic worldview creates a soft and warm flame of passion in us lasting from childhood into adulthood. This flame can either be strengthened, particularity if we are born into an idealistic family or we are surrounded by an idealist who makes an impression on us, and grow to become a real passion we pursue, or dampened and reduced by so-called *nay-sayers* and persons with a different, perhaps more towards a pessimistic, worldview.

Nay-sayers are a prevalent and often an unfortunate phenomenon in our everyday life. A nay-sayer is a person who habitually expresses negative or pessimistic views. Because INFJ «only» constitutes 1%, that goes to say that the potential of disagreeing minds is present and grand. This is, in my opinion, a tragic loss of positive energy and willpower that could serve to change the world, even if just in a small way. However, as we will discuss later in this book; one strong individual can change lives, politics, communities and even leave a grand impact on the world! Consider, for example, strong individuals who have done so much good in this world, like Martin Luther King, Nelson Mandela, and Mother Theresa. It is heartwarming to know that they are considered to be INFJs.

They had a calling inside of them, moving them to action. Despite hardship and resistance from the outside world, they would not allow their inner calling to be silenced or diminished.

Imagine what immense potential there is in us! Each and every one of us has an inner calling and a need fulfill our purpose, serving our community through our unique talents. Our voices need to be heard. We are often individuals with great visions and ideas. However, our nature is to keep them within or within small groups of whom we trust. Therefore, our brilliance might not be shared with the world.

Imagine if people like Thomas Edison didn't share his voice and opinion about creating light. What if he listed to the nay-sayers? What would happen if the founder of Red Cross (Henry Dunant), General and Special Theory of Relativity (Einstein), or Apple (Steve Jobs) agreed with their critics and silenced their inner voice, which continually fed them with motivation to stay strong, go on and continue to change the world, move beyond the current boundaries and use their creative minds to solve an endearing riddle, providing a solution and empowering philanthropy.

INFJs love the luxury of staying anonymous in a big city, allowing our thought to flow freely and ponder on life's great questions without an interception. We adore our wanderlust and love traveling to faraway places, which benefits our chance to flow interestedly through crowds without running the risk of randomly bumping into someone you know or who recognizes you, in which fashion you unwillingly need to pull out your, ever so dreaded, small chat. It is comfortable being anonymous. We love being able to walk around uninterrupted and plainly observe and watch people as they go by. It creates a sense of peace, where there is space for thinking and reflection.

Although we are naturally good at reflection, whilst maintaining a sense of well-being, our brains can sometimes bombard us with thoughts, emotions, and ideas. Walking along a beautiful summers day, we might suddenly get a captivating idea dropping into our heads and getting taken over by it.

Overstimulation happens on a frequent basis. There is so much going on in our heads that we feel overwhelmed by the interaction with someone else. The complex process going on inside our heads may sometimes present a difficulty considering and responding to others feelings and opinions, especially when you are already flooded with yours. The skill to say the right thing, say enough, but not too much, be polite, but stand up for ourselves, can be quite overwhelming. It might feel quite demanding. As we are naturally relatively private and do not feel comfortable by sharing our innermost thoughts like an open book, we don't like to expose ourselves too much. We are therefore conservative in conversations and might not excessively share our personal endeavors. Even if we have walked around pondering on a particular thought all day, we might not say a word about it, even if someone asks us what is on our minds. We feel awkward in revealing ourselves to others unless we are 100% certain they will have our best interests at heart and trust is absolute. They must have proven themselves to be completely loyal, reliant and stable, which might take a long time to achieve. Our gate is usually locked and it takes a particular key to unlock the door to our innermost thoughts. Our biggest fear is to be exposed, even if our thoughts are totally normal and natural, we feel violated if our deepest thoughts and opinions become public. This is why most INFJs would rather skydive from an airplane, than making a speech in front of a crowd of people. Undoubtedly the speech would have been absolutely amazing if we just let ourselves express our authentic opinions and thoughts!

This, however, creates a social paradox for many INFJs. Because we do not trust and open up to others before they prove their loyalties and trustworthiness to us, we are missing out on many very satisfying relationships. Especially with other INFJs, which we so deeply want to connect with, as they too will be reserved in interaction until we show them our trustworthiness. This is a common problem that holds INFJs back from true genuine connection with others.

Furthermore, we are very afraid of criticism and would at times do anything to avoid it. Even if that means blending in with the flowery wallpaper at a social event, so be it! At least we are not exposing ourselves to any threat of being criticized and we are able to preserve status: safe. We are usually neutral in debates as it is regarded as a safe approach. Staying neutral does not require us to be vulnerable, and our perceived safety stays intact. Even if we might burn for the topic discussed and have a clear and to the point opinion just lingering to be heard, we might never open our mouths to say it. Even when a topic we passionately care for comes up for discussion and even if we are asked and our brain is absolutely clear in our opinion, we might leave it to the side for the sake of peace and conflict avoidance. We prefer to be the diplomat; find agreement and compromise between the two parties in discussion. Find similar ground and agree with each other.

However, no rules without the exception. Like anyone, even our peace and harmonic personas will protect ourselves if needed. If we are backed into a corner, metaphorically speaking and we feel threatened and our idealistic views are under scrutiny, then we might raise our voice and speak our minds. When this happens, it has usually been on our minds for quite some time, so the words, arguments, and presentation are well chosen and we are certain to get our point across.

Be aware, cute and kind puppies can also grouse! Don't make us cross, we also know how to defend ourselves. But like some Buddhist, we preserve our skills in battle, only for defense and when needed to save ourselves from a potentially destructive situation. We strive to be righteous, virtuous and to bring justice to any situation. Peace and harmony are one of our highest goals, not only in the exterior world but also the inner world. We praise stillness and peace in our hearts and need time to filter out the negativity that we are exposed to from out outer surroundings. We need to retract, recharge and reset. This is why we retract ourselves and become introverted. The world can be overwhelming. Engaging to long in it without withdrawing to reset ourselves, drains us and leaves us feeling worn out, longing for that beautiful spot alone in wild nature on a picnic blanket, on a grass field with colorful flowers, that wooden dock by the lake or a beach to ourselves, just for a moment, regaining control and mental integrity.

We love to get caught up in fascinating ideas! Nothing can excite an INFJ more than an appealing idea. We are great at seeing the bigger picture, and unlike many other personality types, not so hung up on details. That is, at least not in the start phase of an idea. We are often quite private in exploring these ideas as we know too well that in the start phase of an idea forming in our heads, whether that be business related, a personal project, art or a new career choice, this is where others who do not see the bigger picture like us may rain on our parade, pointing to details in the near future that we yet have not focused on which could stop the whole process going forward. That is why most people don't carry out their ideas and dreams. They see the immediate problems, minor hurdles, and drawbacks that usually are possible to overcome with some troubleshooting and a bit of work. Most won't, but we will. However, since it has not been done before, one will have to think outside of the box, which is where most genius inventions and revolutionizing ideas are created. Every thought inside the box has been thought of already. There is no need to repeat that. Think above and beyond. This creates problem-solving on a higher level. And we are here to live a higher-level life of course.

Have you heard of the amazing theoretical physicist Michio Kaku? He calls himself a futurist and is voting for utopianism, which I find incredibly fascinating and uplifting. His vision is for a greater future and he shows us that contrary to what we learn from the (bad) news in the papers, online and televisions every day, the world is continually becoming a better place to live. If we jumped back 100 years ago, or even 1000 years ago, how would we live? Where there is any legal system protecting the society? Police patrolling the streets, women rights, amnesties or charities? Democracy, neurosurgeons, schools, education, equal rights? We now have the possibility to learn and gather information at our fingertips. There is endless entertainment that comes to you in your own living room through technology and possibility to connect with similar minded INFJs and others all over the world, traveling at the speed people thought to be impossible back in the day, as well as flying airplanes, instant virtual meetings with friends from the other side of the country or world via Skype, Viber, SnapChat or FaceTime.

We have come a long way as humans, both ethically, technologically and financially, and we are creating great things. However, there is no doubt that we still have a way to go still. But how do we get there? From findings by various researchers., there are levels of consciousness where every one person at every point of their lives, find themselves at one level or another. Ascending from the lowest levels of shame, guilt, fear, and hate to include the highest levels of human consciousness which is love, joy, peace and highest of all is enlightenment.

If we are able to see the world or the present moment through love, joy or peace, a new vision of the world arises. When you consciously look for something in particular, you will see more often. This is equivalent to you look for red cars, and you will see them everywhere. If we choose to see love, we will see the loving intention behind a mother's advice, supporting and loving exchanges of words between friends and even people on the street, the loving intention behind our modern technology to create peaceful civilized methods of interaction and travel.

The more you see love, feel love and let love fill your life, the more love you may give to others, similar to a cup filling up with love and therefore loving others from your overflow. And in truth, what does a human being want more in life than being, really, sincerely, deeply seen and loved for who they truly are? Most of all, we need to love and accept ourselves. For who can love others, who do not love themselves? Choose to see life through love, instead of fear.

An elaboration on the topic of fear; have you ever thought about how the media and newspapers often fuel our fear-driven minds with constantly bad news, horrific tragedies, and crimes around the world? Imagine all the small and large acts of peace, love, and altruism that never made the headliners to counterbalance the part of our brain firing up in response to the bad news we just received?

Mindfulness had become quite a beautiful trend and has even entered mainstream psychology practice. Mindfulness is the psychological process of bringing one's attention to the internal and external experiences occurring in the present moment. You can attain this through the practice of meditation and other training. Quieting the chattering mind is the first step to realizing who you truly are. Of course, it isn't possible to completely stop this, but we can definitely begin to soften those thoughts and focus on being more present.

Exploring our authentic selves can be incredibly exciting, and often daunting. Knowing our true core values and beliefs are important for our understanding of our own thinking patterns and behavior. Understanding is the first step towards the possibility of accepting. Having acceptance and compassion for oneself is a true life changer. The inner critic is often our harshest critic, and it is something we all experience, sometimes too well. Displaying loving kindness towards ourselves is transformational in the way we feel, think, live, create, interact, connect and grow. Kindness is an act of love. Self-kindness is the biggest gift you may give yourself. If you haven't already, try a loving-kindness meditation.

2

THE FINE LINE BETWEEN STRENGTH AND WEAKNESS

As an INFJ, there are things you are naturally good at. And at the same time, you also have weaknesses. Your awareness on these two sides of your life is a crucial step in defining who you are.

By understanding yourself, you will know when to proceed with something. You will also know when to pull out. Not only does this lead to happiness, but you'll also be satisfied and grateful for who you are.

Strengths:

There is nothing as good as discovering your strengths and being able to apply them.

Perceptiveness and Intelligence – you are good at seeing through people, situations, and ideas that most others miss. Incredible insight into people and situations. Of all the types, INFJs are most likely to report extreme "psychic" like experiences. You can spot motives before they even mature. For this reason, you are not the type that easily gets manipulated.

Good communication skills – INFJs are good with words. It's no wonder then that they make great writers and public speakers.

INFJs can be great listeners and make those around them feel heard. This allows them to understand others and build rapport very quickly.

Persuasiveness – Because you have great communication skills, you have the power to be persuasive. This is the reason most INFJs make motivating leaders. Examples are Nelson Mandela and Martin Luther King Jr.

Decisiveness – you are not the type that does things for the sake of it. Every activity you pursue must lead to a concrete outcome. And before making a decision, you weigh all options carefully. INFJs commit to finishing what they start. If they take on a project or goal they will focus and work on it until they reach the outcome they're after. INFJs aren't afraid of hard work and your persistence is genuinely inspiring to others.

Like other NFs, INFJs are idealistic. They also tend to be perfectionists...and have the focus to follow through on this idealism. This means they always strive for the best and are often able to deliver it.

Kindness – this is one of the biggest characteristics of all INFJs. You may feel like it's your obligation to make the world a better place. Whenever someone has a problem, you are the type that provides a hand to get him out of the ditch.

Creativity and Artistic – INFJs are good at creating solutions to people's problems. This is the reason they are on the forefront fighting oppression and other societal problems.

Interested in systems and determining the best way to get things done. Couple this with your strong drive to succeed, and you can understand why INFJs are very good at achieving your goals.

Promote Intimate Relationships – when an INFJ gets into a relationship, you can bet it'll stand the test of time. INFJs don't enjoy small talk or one-night stands – they don't get the intimacy they haunt for from such relationships.

INFJs are natural nurturers. They make great parents, spouses, and mentors because they can be patient as well as devoted and protective of those they care about. You will generally form very close and loving relationships while at the same time pushing those you care about to succeed (because of your high expectations).

Highly Developed INFJs Will Enjoy Even More Super Powers:

- Ability to easily turn the understanding of a situation into a plan of action.

- An impressive ability to understand very difficult concepts beyond what your "natural intelligence" would otherwise be able to understand.

- These superpowers often give you as the INFJ an ability to appear "wise" beyond your actual wisdom (although your actual wisdom is often quite impressive).

In summary, a developed INFJ can be:
- Goal Oriented
- Very Driven and Determined

- Persistent
- Insightful
- Creative
- Intelligent
- Logical
- Focused
- Quick
- Caring
- Intuitive
- Supportive
- Inspiring
- Teachers

Keys To Using Your Strengths as an INFJ
- Focus on goals that will bring a balanced happiness to your life.
- Avoid situations ripe with conflict or confrontation.
- Realize you're unique among most groups and learn to accept others (and their weaknesses).

Weaknesses:

You didn't think I was going to stop at your strengths, did you? As much as I say focus on your strengths it is still important to be aware of your weaknesses, even if it is just so you can more easily ignore them.

Below you will find a list of weaknesses, or challenges, common amongst INFJs. As with strengths, this is not a definitive list and do not take it as a prescription for how INFJs have to be.

So if some of these weaknesses don't really resonate with you, good. Ignore them and don't assume you should be weak in that area if you're not. If you do connect with some of the weaknesses, take it as an opportunity to either work to improve that area of yourself, or to accept the weakness and find a solution so you won't have to deal with it.

INFJs' challenges tend to revolve around the tendency to form quick judgments around your values and the values of others. A secondary challenge, tied to the first, is your tendency to find your own value in the perceptions or beliefs of others.

Sensitivity – this is probably the biggest weakness of INFJs. We easily get upset. And this happens even when someone is attacking or criticizing our ideas and not us.

Holding Grudges – you may be able to forgive those who do you wrong. But forgetting is another story. However, holding grudges leads to stress. And it contributes to difficulties in keeping friends.

Too Much Privacy – this makes it difficult for others to connect with you. They never know how you feel or the things you like. And sometimes, they may think they are not good companions.

Striving for Perfection with very high standards and expectations – INFJs like to see that everything as 100% perfect before taking pride in work. But there is one problem with this – it's difficult to achieve perfection. You will find that you are exerting too much effort and feeling exhausted in the end. This can lead to unrealistic (and unfair) expectations of themselves as well as others. Your high expectations of yourself have a positive side effect, your drive, but can also make you be far too hard on yourself. Your high expectations of others can have a motivating effect but can also lead to excessive pressure as well as too much.

You can be very impatient with less intelligent people, or those who disagree with your way of doing things. Conflict and stress can push the INFJ to angry states and ongoing stress often leads to health issues as the INFJ isn't great at dealing with negative states. Can become pigheaded and ignore other people's opinions. This comes from both your mode of operating and interacting with the world, as well as experience. INFJs are very intelligent and perfectionist...so more often than not you are right. INFJs are rarely at peace or 100% happy with themselves or the situation. This positively contributes to your drive but strips them of enjoying the benefits of your hard work as much as you should.

Sometimes you have little regard for what other's think of them. This can lead to offending others, harsh treatment etc.. Can obsess over details that have no real significance to the big picture.

INFJs can be "harsh" in judgments and treatment of other people. This can be seen in different ways including:

- This is especially true if you feel you've been wronged. In this case, you can often hold grudges for far too long and have a lot of trouble forgiving people.

- You can be intolerant and overly judgemental of weaknesses in other people.

- You can get angry or impatient with people who don't "get it" or appear to be doing things wrong.

- You can be very pointed and cruel with your words without regard for the hurt you could cause.

As an INFJ, you can often become ridged in your value judgments, including those of other people and external situations (often without fully understanding a complex situation).

When you become too rigid in your values or way of seeing things you can be overly judgemental of others and become closed off to new possibilities or approaches.

INFJs generally shy away from confrontation. This can lead to tension buildings and unresolved issues lingering in your relationships.

INFJs do not like conflict or confrontation. Life is good when the people around you are happy. This can lead to avoidance behavior and let things bottle up.

INFJs are idealists. You see the world for how it could be and have high expectations of yourself and others. This can lead you to be too hard on yourself and those you care about.

3
FAMOUS INFJs

As an INFJ, you are amongst some very good company. In this chapter, you'll find a collection of famous and "successful" people who are either confirmed or suspected, as being INFJs.

Scientists, Writers and Thought Leaders
- Plato
- Carl Gustav Jung
- Niels Bohr
- Mahatma Gandhi
- Mary Wollstonecraft
- Simone de Beauvoir
- Ludwig Wittgenstein
- Sam Harris
- Dante Alighieri
- Fyodor Dostoevsky
- Alexander Solzhenitsy
- Baruch Spinoza
- Arthur Schopenhauer
- Noam Chomsky

Actors and Performers
- Leonard Cohen
- Marilyn Manson
- George Harrison
- Daniel Day-Lewis
- Al Pacino
- Edward Norton
- Adrien Brody
- Michelle Pfeiffer
- Cate Blanchett
- Carey Mulligan
- Derren Brown

- Rooney Mara

Politicians and Leaders

- Thomas Jefferson
- Calvin Coolidge
- Ron Paul
- Woodrow Wilson
- Marcus Aurelius
- Robert Mugabe
- Osama bin Laden
- Adolf Hitler
- Ayatollah Khomeini
- Leon Trotsky
- Chiang Kai-shek

4
LEARN HOW TO THRIVE AT WORK

There is an astronomical difference between a job you're good at and a career you love and in which you thrive.

While some people are fine just getting by, people like you and I sure aren't. Because you my friend, are an awesome human who has incredible intentions in the world. This section will help you thrive at work.

3 Foundations For Thriving At Work

- Be in the know of your various strengths and weaknesses and be selective of the work you do. Be honest in job interviews about where you excel as well as where you struggle.

- When in a job, take this same honest approach with your supervisor. Explain that you aren't being lazy, rather you feel you could deliver much more value to the company by focusing on your strengths.

- At least once per week, if not daily, stop for a few minutes and ask yourself if you're working in your strengths or struggling in your weaknesses. Remember, you have unique and valuable gifts...but only if you make the effort to use them and avoid getting trapped in the wrong kind of work.

When it comes to your work, be sure to tap into these work-related strengths for INFJs:

- Ability to understand others (empathy).
- Internal drive to achieve goals and be productive. INFJs like making things happen.
- Loyalty and commitment to succeed at work you believe in.
- INFJs have the potential to be excellent mentors and bosses. Your patience, understanding and high expectations of others make you excellent "people developers" who see the potential in others and will work hard to help them grow. Author's note: I Have an INFJ mentor myself and have experienced this first hand - they are awesome.
- INFJs can be logical and rational in how they work yet are also creative. This makes them excellent scientist types who have the ability to "think beyond" current discoveries and come up with new ideas or approaches.
- INFJs are intelligent and have no problem focusing. This gives them an ability to grasp difficult ideas and work on one thing until completion.
- INFJs commit to finishing what they start. If you take on a project or goal you will focus and work on it until you reach the outcome you're after. INFJs aren't afraid of hard work and your persistence is genuinely inspiring to others.
- Interested in systems and determining the best way to get things done. Couple this with your strong drive to succeed, and you can understand why INFJs are very good at achieving their goals.
- Ability to see the big picture and understand the consequences of certain actions or ideas.
- The ability to commit and make 'final' decisions (decisiveness) and solid organizational skills.

To maximize your success, you should be aware of some challenges you may face at work. INFJs will not always, but may:

- Be impatient with people or organizations you see as uncooperative or ineffective. This can play out as the employee feeling smarter than your boss and angry your intelligence and contributions aren't properly rewarded.

- Have difficulty working on projects that conflict with your values.

- Avoid conflict and confrontation, leaving problems unresolved or ignoring unpleasantness or problems that should be addressed.

- Have the reluctance to confront and discipline those they manage.

- Not like competitive work environments because of the inherent tension and conflict you produce.

- Can be stubborn. Once you flex your "decisive" muscle and make a decision you are reluctant to step backward and revisit it.

- Allow your ability to focus and commit can manifest itself negatively as inflexibility.

- Struggle simplifying complex ideas so you can be (quickly) explained to others.

- Have trouble changing plans or direction when the situation calls for it. In other words, in these circumstances, you aren't as adaptable as your other Idealist counterparts.

5
LEARN TO HAVE A HEALTHY RELATIONSHIP

Whoever said opposites attract never met an ENFP + ISTJ couple.

Sure, you want a partner who complements your strengths and weaknesses, but most of us also want someone who understands us; someone with whom we can express our opinions and ideas and be understood.

In this part, we'll discuss what INFJs are like in relationships. Then we'll look at the most common personality types INFJs are happy with. Lastly, we will end with some advice on creating and maintaining successful relationships as an INFJ.

INFJ's IN RELATIONSHIPS

INFJs seek intense and powerful relationships full of romance and meaning. As an INFJ, you demand a lot from your relationships but are willing to give a lot at the same time. Within your romantic relationships as INFJs, you are warm and loving partners.

INFJs tend to buy into the idea of fairytale romance and the existence of a perfect relationship. On a positive note, this belief encourages you to work hard at creating a great relationship. On a negative note, you may be too quick to jump ship when challenges arise. You are loyal and desire a long-term, committed relationship. You are prepared and willing to invest yourself in creating the perfect relationship when you feel you have found the right person.

INFJ's IDEAL MATCHES

A note on compatibility: There is no be-all and end-all. The information on type compatibility is either based on theory or surveys, neither of which will ever provide a universal rule.

NF (idealist) types find the greatest relationship satisfaction dating NFs. This is likely because you can share a common way of thinking and feeling about the world. The two most compatible matches for INFJs are ENTPs and ENFPs.

Ultimately, the two individuals involved, and your desire to grow and work to create an incredible relationship will have the biggest determination of your success together. The one thing incompatibility that I've noticed time and time again is between Intuitives (Ns) and Sensors (Ss). I think this is because these two groups have fundamentally different ways of interacting with the world and often have trouble understanding one another.

TIPS FOR DATING AS AN INFJ

INFJs have a strong dislike of conflict, criticism, and confrontation. You will benefit from developing your ability to handle conflict. The only way to do this is baby steps, one awkward conversation at a time.

INFJs are excellent partners and loyal companions. Value yourself and what you bring to the table. Take time to access those you date and determine if they can match your standards of loyalty of affection.

You may set very high expectations for yourself and your partner. Just remember that everyone is human, and no partner or relationship will be perfect so don't be too hard on your partner, or yourself. And like anything worthwhile in life, great things take time and work.

If you're after a "perfect" relationship take time to check in with your partner on this. Do they share your same high expectations, and if so, is their vision of a "perfect" relationship the same as yours? Communication around these ideas is key to avoiding disappointment.

You may have trouble hitting the eject button on a bad relationship. If your relationship isn't meeting your needs speak to someone you trust for an objective opinion. Your loyalty, caring and desire to make things work could be blinding you to reality.

6
DEALING WITH LONELINESS

You may convince yourself that you are the only one who feels that way. But this problem is more common than you think.

When it comes to establishing relationships, most INFJs feel like they are playing football with a square ball. No matter how hard they try or what tricks they use, it seems so difficult to score.

Reasons why you Feel Alone

Understanding who you are comes with age and experience. And this is also when you get better at controlling your loneliness healthily.

Below are some of the reasons INFJs are usually lonely:

It takes too long to form a relationship: when an INFJ meets a like-minded person, the connection is almost instantaneous. But situations like these are rare. With most people, it takes time to achieve the same level of connection.

While this may not be a problem for you, your friends will take it as disinterest. So, they'll just walk away.

Others can't give as much as you would like in a relationship: Following from the last point, friends may find your need for a deep connection too demanding. And because of their inability to cope with your needs, they'll just withdraw.

You don't open up: INFJs are naturally private people. Unfortunately, others don't take this kindly — especially those who don't understand you. Your reluctance to share your feelings with them can often send signals that you don't trust them. And so, they stop trusting you too.

Sensitivity is also an issue: As you read in Chapter 2, you can be a very sensitive person. Holding grudges makes it difficult to get along with people who cross you.

Your time to recharge is a sign of not wanting to interact: some people see this as a sign of not wanting to interact, so they avoid you.

How you define Loneliness

We make one mistake when talking about loneliness - we generalize it. And this can sometimes backfire as you'll likely fight your loneliness inappropriately.

Physical Loneliness

On some occasions, I've found myself surrounded by people and still discover that I was feeling lonely. This may seem fictitious but it happens to most INFJs. You may feel like this when at a party, work, or anywhere with lots of people.

When most INFJs say they feel lonely, this is the loneliness they refer to. But this isn't what they are actually suffering from.

And you realize this when you start going out to meet new people. You will notice that there is still a hole inside you. In the end, you will find that trying to make lots of friends is exhausting.

Emotional Loneliness

This is the type of loneliness most INFJs suffer from – not feeling connected to other humans. And I've also figured that it's the most important of all to deal with.

You must understand that for an INFJ, quality wins over quantity. You don't need 10 friends to combat emotional loneliness. One friend who connects with you should do.

But then that reminds me of yet another important thing – the solution to loneliness isn't always outside. Sometimes, it's inside you. Once you understand this, you will see that focusing on having lots of friends is a waste of time.

Solutions to Loneliness
There are a number of ways you can use to deal with loneliness. And there is no way I can list everything in this section. Since we are all different, you may discover that some ways work best than others.

Understand Who You Are – you need to acknowledge that you are different. And you must stop trying to be someone you are not. However, this doesn't mean shouldn't make friends. Just don't get caught in establishing friendships. Remember, quality trumps quantity for INFJs.

Here is a little exercise to try – get a piece of paper and a pen. Divide it into two sections. On one side, list the things you love. On the other side, list things you don't like.

You may feel bad about some of the things on your list. But remember, it's just who you are.
For example, a certain INFJ complained that she sometimes avoids people she knows for no apparent reason. Upon further scrutiny, she learned that it was

because she hated small talk, which was just what those people gave her.

Get Out of Your Box – We all need friends. And you won't find them if you sit expecting they will come to you.

You should be the one to make the first move. Just having one or two friends is enough. You will get to enjoy social interactions with normal people and still have time for yourself.

However, you need to be strategic with the type of friends you choose. And even if you choose right, don't expect them to commit to the relationship the way you would want – they may be different from you.

You must also fight your instincts and open up to people you trust. There is no better way to nourish a relationship than this.
Learning to interact is like a training a muscle – it gets better the more you exercise it. With time, you should be able to make a few friends. Some of them will go, but some will stay.

Get a Job – This is the best way to force yourself out of your shell. Getting a job means working alongside other people. You need to, however, go for a job you care about. There is a likelihood of meeting people who have similar interests that way.
Even if you are in a position where you don't need or want a job, it may be of enormous benefit to have one for a social aspect and making some good

connections. This has actually worked wonders for me in the past.

Focus on Making Yourself Happy – By far, this is the most reliable way of fighting loneliness. You must not think that your happiness is under someone's control. It's always in your hands.
You just need to figure out the things that make you happy. Is it music? Helping other people? Or perhaps, writing?

Once you are aware of this, ensure that you make time for it and follow it. Sooner than later, you will discover that focusing on inner happiness beats the need for a friend.

Get a Pet – assuming you get along with animals, owning a pet is a good idea. Having something that breathes curl itself on your lap can make you feel valued. Isn't it amazing how we can trick ourselves into feeling loved by creatures from other species?

7

LEARN TO FIGHT OTHER PEOPLE'S EMOTIONS

Because of the awareness of other people's emotions, it's easy for an INFJ to become an emotional sponge. If these emotions are positive, we become happy. But sometimes, these emotions are negative. And this is a problem since you feel someone's pain or troubles in your heart.

Most INFJs respond to this by avoiding people or situations that subject them to negative emotions. But sometimes, that may not be an option. Besides, you don't need to avoid socializing because you don't want negative emotions.

1. Pinpoint the Emotions
It's easy to mistake someone's emotions as your own. So first, identify if the negative feelings are yours or not.

This knowledge is very important. You will know the source of the emotion, how it affects you, and how you absorb it. Also, it will keep you from overlooking emotions that may be yours and in need of serious solutions.

2. Create an Imaginary Wall
Once you are able to identify negative emotions as they come, you need to imagine that you are

protected by some sort of a shield. I like to imagine being in a glass shell. I can see negative emotions when they hit the glass and fall to the ground.

The only reason this works is that it makes you become conscious of each negative emotion you face. So, you are able to deal with each before it gets into your head.

You can only allow positive emotions to penetrate through your shell.

3. Purge Negative Emotions

Your shell won't be able to block every negative emotion aimed at you. But this is no reason to worry as long as you can identify the ones that get into your head. You can purge them from your body at any time.

There are a couple of ways on how to achieve that. One way is to breathe slowly and imagine the emotion going out as you exhale. Another is to imagine the emotion traveling through your head all the way down into the ground.

4. Avoid Negative Emotions

Prevention is another great medicine against negative emotions. So, if you can, use it.

But first, know the people who give you negative emotions and reduce the time you spend with them. You can come up with excuses to leave a place when they show up. You can say "I don't have much time to talk" and only give them 5 or 10 minutes of your time. Don't force yourself if you know you can't take more.

This doesn't mean suppression of emotions because that would actually be terrible for your well-being. It just means limiting your time with certain people or situations that you know may bring up negative feelings.

5. Give Yourself Space
Although you may socialize like you are not an INFJ, you still need to retreat for some time alone. Remember, you need to recharge your mind. And this "me time" gives you the best chance to get in touch with your feelings. So, use it well.
When in a public place and you get a feeling that you are absorbing negative emotions, seek some space. At a party, for example, you can stand at the edge. In a restaurant, you can choose a table farthest from lots of people. And it helps to look away from them.

6. Plan Your Response to Difficult Situations
Knowing what to say or do before the moment comes can save you from stress. For example, if you have identified people who give you negative emotions, you can plan for what you will do the next time you will meet them.

8
LEARN TO MEET YOUR NEEDS FIRST

From the initial chapters, we know that INFJs are naturally kind people. While this is a good characteristic, it can also be a curse sometimes. As a typical INFJ, you will find yourself helping others all the time at the expense of your own needs.

It has been ingrained in our brains to say "yes" to every request. Serving others is in our DNA, and we may start believing we were born to be helpers. Whenever we think of some "me time," our conscious rushes to dismiss it as selfishness.

Adding to this is the issue of gaining approval from others. And since we aren't always good at keeping friends, we believe that by saying "yes," we'll win some of them into our corner.

So, we end up in situations where our needs always come dead last. Otherwise, any "me time" has to be stolen.

Why It's Important To Meet Your Needs First
Help to others is best served in moderation. Otherwise, by exceeding your limits, you lose it all and get exhausted. And that has several disadvantages in your life.

Here are some of the explanations as to why you should serve yourself first:

You don't sacrifice your own needs – saying "yes" to everything fills your plate with requests from people.

And this leaves you with no time to focus on your needs. Soon, you will discover that a life full of unfulfilled goals becomes meaningless.
You are no different from anyone you help. If you don't make time to focus on yourself, good luck finding someone to focus on you.

You are only useful to others when you help yourself first – you are like a root. Any nutrients you get from the soil will only get to the leaves and fruits if you are in good condition.

If you aren't happy, there is no way you will make anyone else happy. If you are feeling burnt for not giving yourself breaks, you won't have the energy to help anyone else.

You need to think of it in this way – you can't rescue anyone when you are drowning.

You don't get stressed – if you are saying "yes" to more tasks than you can chew, you will build unnecessary pressure. And this will lead to stress, making you feel like a dead man walking.

You prevent frustration – you may be helping people so you can gain their approval. But if your efforts are not being recognized, frustration will set in.
You need to realize that a lot of people don't understand you. But even if there are some that do, their understanding may be limited. You are the only one who exactly knows what goes on inside you. So, you must be at the forefront of ensuring that your needs are being met.

Learning to Put Yourself First

You may not be aware that you are responsible for the way others treat you. And you are also the reason they find it easy to dump all their problems on you. But with some practice, you can also teach everyone around you to see that you need space and help, just like anyone else.

To ensure that your needs are also met:

Determine Your Needs – the first step in this process is figuring out your own needs. Are there any projects you have been neglecting because you were busy taking care of others?
Make a list of all the things you would like to achieve in your life.

Set Priorities – for each of your need, you must give it a priority rating. By doing this, you will always devote your time to the most important things.
Whenever someone asks you to do something, take a moment to think about the consequences of this new task to your planned goals.
And talking about planning, it helps to make a daily schedule. You will find it easier to monitor your progress on how you are meeting your goals.

Set Boundaries – You need to know what you can do for people, how much you can do, and when. You can think of this as taking back your freedom from others.

You must know when to say "no" to people. And when you do it, resist the urge to apologize. Your help is out of kindness, not something anyone buys. It

won't be easy to say this at first, but you will get better at it the more you do it
By saying "no," however, I don't mean you should be rude. You will only go so far with such a behavior. You must explain to people politely that you are unable to help them and give your reasons.

Be ready to make compromises – when you finally master turning down people's requests, don't use your new skill anyhow.

For example, you may have planned to go to the gym for a workout tonight. But if your mom calls telling you she broke a leg and you'll have to take her to the hospital, there is no way you can say "no" to that. Your exercise can certainly wait. Your mother's leg is an emergency and worth missing a workout for.

9
LEARN TO ACHIEVE HARMONY

Achieving harmony is a big issue for most INFJs. Worsening the problem is, we believe that we live in a world where nobody cares about us. As if not enough, we sometimes dedicate much of our time serving others, reducing the time we attend to ourselves.

In the end, our internal struggles intensify. And these destroy our happiness, and sometimes, lead us to unhealthy behaviors.

Without a doubt, everybody has struggled in life. The most important thing is how you get to deal with them. Here are some of the ways you can achieve harmony:

Share your thoughts – because INFJs are private people, this may make you feel uncomfortable. But opening up to others has a number of benefits.

When you tell others your troubles, they may help you come up with solutions. And in some cases, these people may be the source of the troubles. It's only when you communicate that they will realize their mistakes. Not only that, but people will feel and respect your authenticity and vulnerability.

But even if the people you tell don't find solutions or are not the source of your problems, it's a huge relief to tell someone what's bothering you.

Before you start sharing your worries, you need some people you can trust. These can be your family or you can make friends with people you respect. The ENFP personality is a good example of friends as they are authentic.

Meditate – if you have been neglecting this, then you have been missing out. Meditation relaxes both the mind and the body. It makes you see life positively, bringing happiness and meaning to it.
Even if you are a busy bee, you should easily fit meditation into your day. Just 15 minutes is enough to rejuvenate you.

Stop worrying about the future – almost everyone worries about the future. But I like to think that INFJs cross the line. We like to believe that life will be miserable forever. Little do we realize that this brings fear and erodes happiness.

By worrying, you don't solve even a single problem. You actually waste time that you would have used to make the future better. So, every time you start to worry, stop and focus your energy on something productive.

Stop criticizing yourself – because you strive for perfection, you will likely criticize yourself whenever you fail. Not only does this bring morale down, but you will also be afraid to try things for fear of failure. Acknowledge the fact that no one can achieve perfection. It's the reason people say "there is always room for improvement." Stop beating yourself for little flaws.

When setting goals, ensure that they are achievable. If you've never worked for 13 hours a day before, it's stupid to think you will do it now. You will surely end up with mediocre results.

Forgive and forget – you must learn to see things objectively. Getting upset by every joke will make it hard to keep friends. Also, it means you will be carrying grudges against almost everyone.
Holding grudges, however, is like being tied to a chain. You can't move on by keeping things that happened in the past. You also can't find happiness. Learn to forgive – you will only do yourself a favor. But then, forgivingness is easier said than done. Just practice sitting down and think of the grudges you have. Now imagine each one getting out with your carbon dioxide as you exhale.

Another trick is to hang out more with the people you are mad at. By having a good time with them, all the tension will automatically dissolve.

Give thanks – with stress blurring the mind, it becomes difficult to think of anything good. This is where "giving thanks" comes in.

Get a paper and note down all the things you are thankful for in your life. Spend time on each and think of how it makes you happy.

For example, if you've just opened a shop, making your first sale is a reason to smile about.
You can celebrate anything you value. It could be your job, your life, your significant other, etc. These exercise releases feel-good hormones. Finding gratitude in your daily life is proven to improve your overall health and state of well-being. And it is

impossible to be in a negative state at the same time we are in gratitude.

Remember fitness – anger and stress are energies. If you don't spend them on something, they control every move you make.

Physical activity or simple workouts are a good way to reduce these energies. Additionally, it also releases the feel-good hormones. You can run, walk, do push-ups, lift weights, ride a bicycle or do any exercise you know.

Sleep – this refreshes and energizes your body. The recommendation is that you should aim for at least 6 hours of sleep daily. But you shouldn't exceed 8 hours.

For even better results, try to go to bed at the same time. Also, you must eliminate destructions. This specifically refers to your phone – switch it off. During the day, take naps when you feel tired. This will make you more productive.

Laugh – this is life's best medicine for happiness. Even better, you don't always need a friend to laugh. You can watch movies, read jokes, or just laugh at nothing (make sure you are alone if you decide to laugh at nothing. Otherwise, people will think you have gone crazy).

Eat right – since food is the body's fuel, you must get enough of it all the time. Enough of the right stuff, of course. Not all food is good for your body – you must only eat the right food. And it must be only what you need. Focusing on fresh, natural, local, organic foods where possible. That will guarantee good healthy (very important as you can only deal with problems when you are fit).

10
CONCLUSION

Vast, expansive and unchained: this describes the creative thought processes of the INFJ. Guided by impeccable clarity and intuition, INJFs range far and wide across unbounded mental horizons, shining their special light of illumination into every nook, cranny, and shadow that might conceivably shelter an important insight. The intellectual tools of inference, projection, and synthesis are like putty in the hands of these vibrant and original thinkers, and because INFJs combine their mental wizardry with an unquenchable belief in limitless possibility, they are masters at creating original solutions to problems that others would consider unsolvable. INFJs are idealists and dreamers, it is true; however, they back it up with a rock-solid ability to translate their savviest inspirations into high-quality real-world strategies for change and improvement.

We are all familiar with the process by which a caterpillar morphs into a butterfly, but if we were to imagine an amorphous creature that continually shifts back and forth from caterpillar to butterfly depending on the requirements of the seasons, we might have an equivalent metaphor for the way INFJs are able to move from the theoretical to the practical and back again as needed. Introversion aside, INFJs live for the opportunity to constructively interact with their society. Whether they are solving problems on the job, joining activist movements striving to bring about concrete social change, mentor or counselor to those in need of moral support and expert assistance, INFJ's are keen to help.

In their temperaments and spirits, INFJs are very much involved in this world, and they are constantly looking for ways to improve it and the lives of all its inhabitants, including themselves. When empathy and intelligence are intermingled, the results can be spectacular, and INFJs are living proof that big dreams are the cornerstones of noble ambitions, loving interrelations, and tremendous personal achievement.

Note from the author

Thank you for purchasing and reading this book. If you enjoyed it or found it useful then I'd really appreciate it if you would post a short review on Amazon. I do read all the reviews personally so that I can continually write what people are wanting.

If you'd like to leave a review then please visit the link below:

https://www.amazon.com/dp/B0746KD5F3

Thanks for your support and good luck!

Check Out My Other Books

Below you'll find some of my other books that are popular on Amazon and Kindle as well. Simply visit the links below to check them out.

Below you'll find some of my other books that are popular on Amazon and Kindle as well. Simply search the titles listed below on Amazon.

Alternatively, you can visit my author page on Amazon to see other work done by me.

ENFP: Understand and Break Free From Your Own Limitations

INFP: Understand and Break Free From Your Own Limitations

ENFJ: Understand and Break Free From Your Own Limitations

ENFP: INFP: ENFJ: INFJ: Understand and Break Free From Your Own Limitations – The Diplomat Bundle Series

INTP: Understand and Break Free From Your Own Limitations

INTJ: Understand and Break Free From Your Own Limitations

ENTP: Understand and Break Free From Your Own Limitations

ENTJ: Understand and Break Free From Your Own Limitations

ISTJ: Understand and Break Free From Your Own Limitations

OPTION B: F**K IT - How to Finally Take Control Of Your Life And Break Free From All Expectations. Live A Limitless, Fearless, Purpose Driven Life With Ultimate Freedom

Made in United States
North Haven, CT
07 October 2023

42464392R00032